In remembrance of

Linda Diane Caldwell

That Crow
That Visited
Was Flying Backwards

John Brandi

Tooth of Time
Books
1984

Some of these poems have appeared in present or earlier versions in:
The Greenfield Review, White Pine Journal, Trapani Nuova (Sicily),
& in previous books by *Doggeral Press, Tooth of Time, Whistling
Swan,* and *Painted Stork Publications.*

ISBN: 0-940510-05-7

This second printing of *That Crow That Visited Was Flying Backwards* contains selected "hoops" from the first edition, along with excerpts from two earlier books: *Sky Hourse* and *At The World's Edge.* The illustrations are mostly new, some taken from Asian journals, others from jottings back home. I've referred to the poems as "hoops" because they are assembled chronologically from autumn to autumn in a year's cycle; and because the book represents a journey—physical, emotional— from New Mexico high deserts to Khumbu Himal, Nepal, and back again. Ultimately, these poems are from my own continent, the heart. It is my hope that they provide an alternative to longer, less compact verse that often miss the quick flashes of the mind as it comes full-circle through geography.

The Japanese have a saying: "The world turns through partings." I remember the irony of finding myself halfway around the world from people I'd left behind only to have come nearer to them in the distance. I was following a trail up past Buddhist monasteries along the Dudh Kosi River toward the base of Mt. Everest. In the end, there was only sky, silence. A stranger on the way remarked, "Here you can go no higher. It is as if you have already left heaven behind."

John Brandi

Tesuque, New Mexico
Spring, 1984

That Crow
That Visited
Was Flying Backwards

October frost:

first fire, & the last
of the flowers
　　—into a single
　　　vase.

Went to the river
again—

That place
we used to sit
    swcpt away.

My neighbor's house
moves a little closer
    —this cold
        autumn night.

9

Waterbirds
turn in the rain

I stop
now & then, to miss you
   —& to pretend.

Kept it to myself
for so long
I forgot what it was
I wanted to say.

How it ought to be.
How it is.

Once again,
it's up to me.

China tea,
gingered vegetables:

not as good as I thought,
eating here alone.

Shirt ironed,
hair tied back—

But wine on my breath
this early in the morning
gives it all away.

Alone with
his books, the
scholar

farts . .

The intellect
at its best:

clowning.

Left those clothes
flapping on the line
for a week now
      —just to have
         company.

The kitten
is the first to hear
my latest poem

No applause
No criticism

Not such a bad
audience   —the apple
                    orchard

Blown sideways
in tonight's wind

    —the moon's halo

You're here
but the wine I'd saved
is gone.

Pretending
there's nothing to say
says everything.

I've come this far
only to know
that knowing isn't enough.

The grass:
flattened in the sun
where we argued.

You know, I know
Maybe we both
know something different

I try so hard
there's not a single poem
to write

Saying no
so many times, it begins
to sound like yes

"Come back!"
my hermit-friend says

"You forgot your
       footprint."

More stable than mine
—the sparrow's
home.

The woodpeckers
too
are at work on my house

Again
busy with poems
instead of firewood

Such pleasure
in the hiss of green wood
I choose to freeze.

All these
gray hairs . .

Now maybe people
will believe me?

Blew all
my money, trying
to save it.

Even my father
says I'm
looking old.

This first day
of spring

The polywog
is the biggest animal
in the world.

A true test
of what I've learned:

these flies
the summer heat!

More crows than ever
now that he's put up
the scarecrow.

Dusk:

a lunar moth
datura slowly opening
& the neighbors
　　　—arguing.

Crickets sing
to teach
the breeze.

Searching for the key;
there in my pocket
all the time.

Wrong side
of the road again

—following
the Morning Star.

Wanted her as goddess
Wanted her as mother

Somehow missed
everything in between.

Feel small enough
to fit through that door
I could never enter.

Where is a word
for this?

How it happens
      along the way

                                    Just as I put my
                                    foot down,   a sparrow
                                          flies up—

The cry
of the killdeer:

I am even farther from you
this spring evening.

Now that you're gone
everything I wanted to say
comes back

Moved into place
by what I thought
I moved out of place

Neither yours
nor mine, those shadows
behind us.

Bound in knots
by what we thought
we let go of.

Whenever I begin
my poems
   —the mosquitoes swarm

Unable to say
farewell
like we said hello

Snow geese
cross the red moon;
a cricket climbs my toe
   —& begins to sing

Everytime I write
—she's there
again.

Whenever I begin
my poems
   —the mosquitoes swarm

Unable to say
farewell
like we said hello

Snow geese
cross the red moon;
a cricket climbs my toe
   —& begins to sing

Look for me
in that maze of canyons
that won't stop
its call.

So tired
my shadow moves
faster than me

Piled side by side
as I top the pass

—prayer stones
& yak dung

Not on top
Not at the edges

But right in the middle
of the fir tree
—the crow lands

34

Yun Han above
Dudh Kosi below

    —river of stars
    —river of milk

I grow smaller
  in between

The proper language
in these mountains:

only a wink
from the first passerby
in four hours

The schoolboy from
Kumjung

    —his bookbag decorated
    with tampons

So clear
the moon rises in front
of the clouds

Standing above canyons
afraid to write poems
about canyons

Pagodas, and
gold doorways

    —but it's the radish vendor
    that fascinates him most

After last night's
blizzard

    —only the sound
    of a water-driven prayerwheel

Poems
like stones, standing
    still   in the river's
            middle

For a moment
thought I was approaching
another village

    —the smell of woodsmoke
      from my own clothes

"Mind your head"
  —a sign above a doorway

But I go on
minding only the heart.

Just as moonlight
reaches the monastery
monks file out to the latrine.

40

Tonight
the dog's barking
is not of this world

Naturally
a raven would be perched
there:

    the broken bridge.

The cook
slips noodles into the soup
with the same hand
she used to blow her nose

The innkeeper
tries to clean the hearth
while the fire's
    still burning.

Farther I journey
closer I am
to ones left behind.

Somebody greater
than God
is responsible for this:

the Pleiades
rising exactly in line
with Everest's tip

Journeyed all this way
to hear a Frenchman say:

"It looks like
National Geographic"

The silence
    made greater
by a distant tumbling
    of stones . . .

All those poems
that got away
live in a deeper place now

Bats
in the Buddha's ears!

Even yesterday
is too far back
to remember

47

No backwards,
no forwards

in the November
rain.

Looking for
a better way in
I travel back roads
      out—

                        Most often
                        the two feet below me
                        step in my way

Somewhere
between wanderer & homemaker
  —find a place to live

49

12,000 miles
I carried that bottle
of musk

    —& gave it
      to the wrong woman.

Rain

  beating into itself
  beating into itself

    across the lake

Because the heart knows
I go against what
the mind thinks best.

At sea

No word
for the deepness

The line goes down
forever

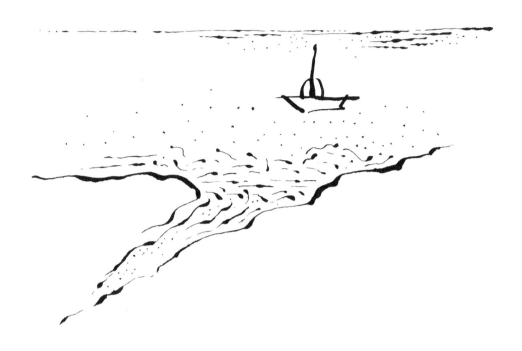

Waiting for you
I dream
of a boat at a river's mouth:

no sail
no oar

The year stands still.

That crow
that visited
was flying backwards

So close
but my deepest thoughts
are spoken elsewhere

Here I am now
Here you are now

Just this.

The end of the road
is what started
it all—

An edition of 500 copies set in 10 point
Trump using Warren's Antique Book Paper
printed by West Coast Print
Center & published by
Tooth of Time Books
634 E. Garcia
Santa Fe
New Mexico
87501

*

We encourage bookstores
to order direct from our distributors:
Book People: 2929 Fifth St., Berkeley, Ca. 94710
Inland Book Co.: P.O. Box 261, East Haven, Ct. 06512
Bookslinger: 339 E. Ninth, Saint Paul, Minn. 55101
S.P.D.: 1784 Shattuck Ave., Berkeley, Ca. 94709